Handpainted Eggs

MONIKA MÜLLER

δελος

CAPE TOWN

© 1993 Tafelberg
28 Wale Street, Cape Town

Also available in Afrikaans as *Handgeverfde Eiers*

Photography by André Stander
Illustrations by Martingraphix
Cover and book design by Debbie Odendaal
Typography by Alison Stander
Typeset in 10 on 12pt New Century Schoolbook by Martingraphix
Printed and bound by National Commercial Printers, Goodwood

First edition 1993

ISBN 1-86826-261-8

Contents

Introduction

For thousands of years people have been fascinated by the unique form of the egg. The various shapes of birds' eggs – from round to oval – are pleasing to the eye, and the egg itself is interesting because of its rich symbolic associations. In almost every human culture the egg symbolizes life, hope, resurrection, growth and the future. The art, folklore, mythology and religion of most cultures accord the egg particular importance.

EGGS IN ART

Many famous artists, from Albrecht Dürer to Pablo Picasso, have used the egg as a subject in their paintings. Apart from being incorporated into works of art, this fragile object has been reproduced by artists and craftsmen. Gold, stone, silver, wood, porcelain, wax, papier-mâché and glass are just some of the materials from which eggs have been made over the centuries. In addition, all kinds of interesting and difficult techniques have been applied to them.

Porcelain manufacturers the world over have produced the most exquisite and delicate eggs, while gold- and silversmiths have created opulent and artistic silver and gold eggs enhanced with enamel work. In 18th-century Russia it was particularly fashionable in wealthy aristocratic circles to give jewelled eggs as gifts. Fabergé and Ovchinnikov are two Russian goldsmiths that achieved international fame for their opulent jewelled eggs. Fabergé's extremely valuable and lavishly decorated eggs, produced for the Russian royal family, have not been equalled by any other goldsmith. His creations mirrored the wealth of the Russian aristocracy at the turn of the century. Ovchinnikov's famous creations, especially his so-called cloisonné enamel pieces, earned him his first gold medal in 1865.

Other artistic egg creations include those of the glass-blowers of Italy, stunning carved wooden eggs from China and beautiful painted wooden eggs from India and South America, to name just a few.

THE EGG-PAINTING TRADITION

Just as ancient as the art of producing decorative eggs from a wide variety of materials is the custom of decorating real eggs (after the contents of the egg have been removed!) and giving them as gifts. Legend has it that Mary, the mother of Jesus, started this custom when she presented her newborn son with red, yellow and green eggs. However, it is likely that this practice goes even further back into history.

The ancient folk art of egg painting is enjoying a revival, and with it the charming custom of giving painted eggs as presents on special occasions. These eggs can be decorated using a multitude of different techniques, some of which are described in this book. Decorated or undecorated eggs can also be inscribed with a verse or message conveying the giver's feelings. The egg itself is a powerful symbol, and decorated with another symbol it assumes even more significance. A personalized egg is certainly a most unusual gift.

Eggs are most commonly associated with Easter, and while the chocolate egg is now a more common Easter gift than a hand-painted egg, many people still decorate their own eggs and hand them out at Easter, particulary to children. Traditionally people made eggs for many different occasions besides Easter. For example, in some European countries women like to hide painted eggs in their baby's cradles to ensure luck and prosperity for the new offspring. In traditional Chinese families it is customary to paint eggs red to announce birth.

In some parts of Europe, girls paint eggs to give to their sweethearts, especially at Easter. The young man receiving the most eggs is regarded as the most eligible bachelor in the village. It is believed that he will marry the girl whose egg has not faded the following year. In other parts of Europe lovers send eggs to each other with loving verses, sayings or mottoes. But eggs have also been used to express dislike. If a lover transferred his affections elsewhere, the egg was dashed to the floor to indicate despair.

In certain parts of Europe eggs are commonly painted with slogans or messages and given to family members and friends on special occasions. In some cases, a ribbon or printed banner is attached to the egg.

The many examples of painted eggs in the folk museums of Europe show how much effort people went to in bygone days to produce a work of art that would convey their feelings for the recipient.

I hope this book will inspire you to try egg painting yourself and rediscover the joy that many people in the past found in creating – and giving – a work of art on the shell of an egg. The techniques are explained as simply as possible so that anyone can follow them, whether they are talented or not.

Preparation

BASIC EQUIPMENT

Before you start you will need a selection of eggs, blowing equipment, natural or chemical colouring ingredients, brushes and finishes (which vary according to the type of decorating you intend to do).

More specialized equipment will be mentioned in the descriptions of the various techniques, where appropriate.

The well-prepared egg painter has the following at hand:

- A vacuum pump or syringe
- A variety of eggs
- A variety of pens, including felt-tipped (koki), white and ballpoint
- Acrylic paint: artist's, poster or Bauernmalerei
- Adhesive tape
- Artists' brushes (numbers 0, 1, 2 and 3)
- Calligraphy pens (Rexel numbers 2, 3 or 5 are available at most stationery shops)
- Carbon or graphite paper
- Cooking oil
- Curtain rings
- Egg containers
- Ingredients for natural colouring, if this is to be used (see p. 6)
- Matchsticks
- Methylated spirits or vinegar to clean the outside of the shells
- Nib pen for etching
- Palette (this could be a tile or a saucer)
- Patina set (this consists of a tube of burnt umber artist's oil colour, a bottle containing one part linseed oil mixed with two parts turpentine and a cloth for application)
- Pins
- Round file
- Scissors
- Script brush (for calligraphy)
- Small wooden skewers (sosatie sticks)
- Sponge
- Spray varnish
- Threads and ribbons
- Toothpicks
- Tracing paper
- Water to rinse out the eggs

CHOOSING THE EGGS

It is worth taking some trouble to choose the right eggs before you start decorating. Look out for eggs with strong, stain-free shells. Chicken eggs are the cheapest and easiest to find, and farm eggs are the best. Choose eggs with white shells, because they show off the background colour beautifully. Brownish eggs are suitable for designs with dark backgrounds, or if you will not be doing a painted background.

If you are planning to display the decorated eggs together it is more interesting if you have a variety of shapes and sizes, so try to get hold of some other types, such as geese, duck and turkey eggs. The world's largest egg – that of the ostrich – has beautiful natural tones. Duck eggs have an attractive porcelain-like appearance, but do not take colour easily. Geese and ostrich eggs are very robust, but their surfaces often have to be sanded down before you can paint on them. Take all these factors into consideration when choosing an egg for a particular design.

EMPTYING THE EGGS

It is essential to get rid of the contents of the egg, especially if you intend giving it away or keeping it for a long time. Eggs that are boiled and then painted should be eaten within a few days, otherwise they will start to smell. Make sure that an egg prepared in this way doesn't have any cracks, however fine, or the egg will go off and a very nasty smell will result.

There are two ways of removing the contents of the egg:
- By mouth
- With a vacuum pump or syringe

By mouth: Pierce the egg with a pin at both ends. Then carefully 'drill' larger holes about 2,5 mm in diameter at these positions, using a round file. Stir the contents with a toothpick to break the yolk, then blow carefully through one hole, holding the egg over a bowl to catch the contents. Do not use eggs straight out of the fridge, since the shells are fragile and will break more easily. Ideally they should be at room temperature.

With a vacuum pump or syringe: For this method you

need make only one hole, about 2,5 mm in diameter, at one end of the egg. Hold the egg over a bowl with the hole facing downwards. Force air into the egg through the hole, and the contents will start coming out. Continue until the egg is empty. Because a slight pressure builds up inside the egg during this process, the shell will break if it is too thin or if it is cracked.

CLEANING THE EGGS

It is essential to rinse the egg out thoroughly to prevent odours. Fill the pump or syringe with warm water and inject it into the egg. Shake the egg for a moment and repeat the procedure. Dry the egg in a warm, sunny place.

BASIC BACKGROUNDS

In most cases you will need to do a basic groundcoat or background on your egg before applying the 'artwork' to it.

There are two main ways of colouring eggs:
○ Natural colouring with plant colours
○ Chemical colouring with any PVA, acrylic, enamel or watercolour paints

Natural colouring

It is particularly satisfying to dye eggs the traditional way, with natural colouring agents such as leaves, roots, flowers and onion skins.

If you take a good look round your house and garden you will find many substances and plants that will yield suitable colours.

Here is a list of some of them:
○ For yellow shades: saffron, lemonwood, camomile blossoms
○ For brown shades: oak bark, coffee, tea, onion skins
○ For green shades: stinging nettles, spinach
○ For reddish shades: beetroot, red cabbage, onion skins with vinegar, red flowers
○ For blue shades: blue flowers, blueberries, elderberries

Method

1　Wipe the egg with vinegar to remove all traces of dirt. It must be clean and free of any grease before the background colour is applied, or it will take the dye unevenly.
2　To prepare the dye, boil the ingredient of your choice until the water is the shade you want. Strain it

through a piece of cloth and add a little vinegar to make the colour more luminous.
3　Next, put the eggs in the hot colour bath. If you want pastel tones, leave them in for a short while only. The longer you leave them, the deeper the shade will be.
4　The empty eggs may float so it is essential to submerge them with a spoon or let them fill up with the liquid. Remember to empty them with a syringe afterwards! Carefully rinse the dyed eggs and allow them to dry thoroughly.

Chemical colouring

Chemical fabric dyes offer a much greater variety of rich, beautiful shades than natural dyes and, although ready-made prepacked dyes are expensive, they are easy to use.

Bear in mind that some of them are poisonous, but this should not be a problem if you intend to use the egg for decoration only.

Special dyes for Easter eggs are available in South Africa in specialist German bookshops, delicatessens and coffee shops. They are inexpensive and easy to use.

Generally, ready-made dyes are used in the same way as natural dyes; the eggs simply have to be soaked in them.

BRUSHING ON BACKGROUND COLOUR

A quick and easy way to apply a groundcoat to the egg is to brush on any kind of ordinary PVA or acrylic, poster or watercolour paint. Oil and enamel paints are seldom used.

Use bright colours for your backgrounds, and experiment by mixing colours to obtain unusual effects. Black, brown and white also make excellent groundcoats.

Remember the following colour combinations:
○ Red and yellow = orange
○ Red and white = pink
○ Red, white and a little green = off-pink
○ Red and blue = purple
○ Red and a little blue = carmine red
○ Red and a little ochre = vermilion
○ Yellow and blue = bright green
○ Yellow and black = dark olive green
○ Blue and a little white = light blue
○ Blue and green = greenish or Danish blue

Method

1　Slide a wooden skewer (sosatie stick) or a needle

through the clean, blown egg to hold it while you paint.
2 Carefully apply the groundcoat with a suitable brush.
3 Allow the egg to dry. You may need to apply several coats to obtain a smooth finish.

DIVIDING UP THE SURFACE

Give some thought to the way you intend to space your designs. Start by dividing the egg into halves with an ordinary or white pen – horizontally or vertically. You could also draw a circle or medallion shape on each side. This will help you make the most of the unique shape of the egg in your design.

TRACING, COPYING AND DRAWING MOTIFS

If you find a motif you would like to transfer onto your egg, either in this book or elsewhere, trace it on a sheet of tracing paper. Use a pencil so you will be able to make changes if you want to.

Cut the tracing paper to roughly the same shape as the egg, then put a piece of carbon or graphite paper under the pattern, securing the pattern to it with a piece of adhesive tape.

Trace over the design with a ballpoint pen to transfer it to the surface of the egg. Of course, if you are confident enough in your drawing ability, you can draw the design straight onto the egg.

Paint techniques

MARBLING

A marbled effect looks stunning on an egg, and is easy to obtain. You can paint the effect on the surface or roll the egg in a colour bath.

Method 1

When marbling with a brush, the technique is to apply two contrasting layers of acrylic paint. Use strong, contrasting colours such as red and green, blue and orange, pink and green, yellow and blue or the classic black and white.
1   Once the first coat has dried, it may need a light sanding to produce the smooth surface characteristic of marble.
2   Paint on the second, contrasting, coat with swirling movements of the brush, and while it is still wet distress and soften it with a squeezed sponge or a dry brush, taking off more colour in some areas than in others.
3   Finally add 'veins' with a brush (number 0 or 1). Paint the 'veins' first in the darker shade, then quickly soften with a sponge or brush; add the lighter 'veins' and soften again before the paint dries completely.
4   Apply one of the finishes (p. 26) to add lustre.

Method 2

For this method you need wallpaper paste, mixed according to the instructions on the package and poured into a bowl.
1   Taking extreme care, pour small amounts of enamel paint on top of the paste so it 'floats' like the cream on top of milk.
   Swirl the paint gently with a toothpick or wooden skewer to create slight movement, but don't mix the paint into the paste.
2   Place the blown egg on top of the skewer and balance the stick on the edges of the bowl, lightly rolling it until the whole surface of the egg is covered.
3   Then rest or suspend either side of the stick on or from something so that the egg lies in a horizontal posi-

tion, and leave it for 12 to 24 hours until quite dry.
4   To produce the characteristic sheen of real marble, apply a drop of cooking oil or use spray varnish.

RAGGING

1   Apply two contrasting layers of acrylic paint to the surface, but before the second coat is dry use a twist of muttoncloth or newspaper to distress the surface with a twirling movement. Ragging produces a subtle but interesting effect.
2   Apply one of the finishes (p. 26) to add lustre.

SPONGING

This is a quick and easy way to obtain a beautiful background.
1   Allow the first layer of paint to dry, then wet a sponge (preferably a natural one), squeeze out the water and dip into a contrasting colour.
2   Sponge lightly over the surface, and apply one of the finishes described on p. 26 to add lustre.

COLOUR PANELS

Eggs can look striking if decorated simply with different colour panels. To obtain this effect, have two or three different colour baths ready, made from prepacked dye kits.
1   Pull a skewer through the egg and dye just one part or panel of the egg, then let it dry and then dip it into another colour, allowing the two colours to blend slightly at the edges. Repeat this two or three times until the egg is completely coloured.
2   Allow it to dry and then highlight the lines between the colour panels with a fine brush in either white or dark-brown paint.
3   Finish off according to one of the techniques described on p. 26, to add lustre and to protect your work.

Bauernmalerei and folk art

These are very traditional methods of decorating eggs. Bauernmalerei is a charming folk art with a naive and unpretentious style, dating back to the 15th century. It was originally practised by farmers and cabinet-makers in many European countries but especially in Austria, Switzerland, Germany, the Netherlands and Norway.

The touch is unskilled and the paint applied with typical bold brush strokes. Favourite motifs are flowers, birds, genre scenes as well as lettering, and they are seldom true to nature but rather simplistic and abstract. The colours are strong but never garish. The main flowers are the tulip, carnation, four- and multi-petalled marguerite and, in particular, the rose. Alpine or exotic flowers are never used.

Vases, baskets or jugs are often added to the floral design. The lay person may regard the motifs of Bauernmalerei as mere embellishment, but in fact they have symbolic meanings handed down from one generation to the next. Most are of pagan origin but over time obtained a Christian significance. For instance, the rose symbolizes Christ, the tulip the flame in Christ and the carnation the nails in the hands of Christ.

THEMES AND MOTIFS

Suitable themes for folk art are one or more flowers, bouquets, flower baskets, hearts and birds. You can use one side of the egg to write a message, for example an Easter greeting or a verse, and you should always include the date.

Make sure your design is simple and not too contrived. Remember that in this case 'less is more'.

Materials

Acrylic paint in tubes or little jars (suitable for Bauernmalerei, poster, Plaka)
Brushes (number 1, 2 or 3)
Tracing materials
Prepared eggs

Method

1 Take a prepared egg, carefully slide a skewer or needle through it and apply the groundcoat with a household brush. You may need several coats for a smooth foundation.

2 Use bright colours for the groundcoats, and if you have the confidence don't be afraid to experiment a little, mixing the colours for more variety. You can even use marbling, sponging or ragging to obtain unusual background effects, and a black or white background can also look interesting. You don't have to stick to red, yellow and blue!

3 After the groundcoat has dried, sand it to prepare it for the decorative work. Choose your patterns from the selection given on p.31. Once you have decided on a design, trace it onto the egg as described on p. 7. Experienced folk-art painters usually draw the design directly onto the egg with a white pencil.

4 You may decide to use two motifs, one on either side of the egg. In this case your first step is to divide the egg into halves with a pen.

5 Get your paints ready on your palette. Make sure you have a glass of water at hand to clean the brushes, as well as a piece of damp cloth to wipe them.

6 Using a fine brush (number 1, 2 or 3) first paint the flowers and then the leaves. To achieve a lively effect always mix your colours by dipping the brush into different colour blobs of paint. Paint wet on wet, and highlight the edges of leaves and petals in white. Work from top to centre.

7 Decorate your roses, tulips, carnations and marguerites with lots of dots and commas in white; these serve to highlight the motif. Dark-brown or black commas will soften the design.

8 Leaves on dark backgrounds should be painted in light green with some white and ochre. On light backgrounds, leaves should be painted in rich dark green, using black and yellow or black and ochre.

9 Paint features such as birds, roosters, hens and hearts as fancifully as you like with wings, crests and tails formed by decorative brushwork.

10 Separate the designs on either side of the egg with borders of commas, dots, tiny daisies or any other border design.

11 When one side is finished, allow it to dry by placing the egg on an egg carton, or letting it hang from a thread.

12 When it is completely dry, decorate the other side.

13 The finished egg may be lightly patinated (see p. 26) to obtain the traditional appearance.

Naive painting

In a world in which pessimism and anxiety are often uppermost, the naive painter expresses honesty, spontaneity, delight and happiness in his work. Naive art also reacts against today's high-tech society, perfectionism and an overly rational way of thinking. Many people are confused about the term 'naive', thinking it has the same meaning as 'primitive' because of its ingenuousness and the fact that it does not adhere to strict artistic rules.

Since the middle of the 19th century naive art has been an established genre all over the world. It should not be confused with folk art, which has been carried on by tradition as a custom in different countries.

The naive painter is usually a 'Sunday artist', and his weekday work bears little resemblance to his naive productions. On these he can work without being worried or influenced by intellectual trends, expressing his dreams of a safe world and inviting us to share them.

THEMES AND MOTIFS

You can allow your imagination free rein when it comes to choosing these. When I do naive pictures I tend to include elements of the little village in which I spent my childhood. The river and the small chapel are always there, as are my favourite animals and of course the trees: an apple tree, a tree in flower and a tree with a little house in the background. Then there are the people, dressed in national costume or selling flowers in the market.

Materials

White acrylic paint for groundcoat
Brushes (number 0, 1 or 2)
Pencil (if drawing freehand)
Tracing materials
Muttoncloth
Patina set
Prepared eggs

Method

1   First paint the area in which you intend to paint the naive picture in white, with two coats if necessary. It may be round, square or oval in shape. The rest is painted in the colour of your choice.

2   When the white groundcoat has dried, trace your chosen pattern on it as described on p. 7, or draw freehand with pencil. Whichever method you choose, concentrate first on the larger outlines of the motif, drawing for example the trees but not the leaves or the fruit.

3   The next step is to paint the sky in varying blue tones, with white patches for the clouds. Soften the effect with a piece of muttoncloth, dabbing off some colour to produce an interesting finish. The clouds should be painted more thickly than the surrounding sky.

4   Now paint the hills, mountains and meadows in different green tones and allow the paint to dry.

5   Paint the apple tree in various green tones and, once it has dried, paint it again in different shades.

6   Then add the apples and all other details, for example a few birds in the sky, and some flowers and grass on the ground.

7   The edges of the picture may be rounded off with commas or dots. With a fine brush (number 0) and black or white paint, add finishing touches to the tiny commas, lines and dots.

8   On the other side of the egg you may paint the date and a few commas or leaves.

9   If you are putting people into your picture, do the groundcoat and the tracing as described above, and then paint the faces and the arms. Complete all the other parts in whatever colours you like.

10   The finishing touches are done with a very fine brush in black and white. Note that the lines on the face should be as simple as possible. Little details may change the whole expression in a very charming way.

NAIVE LANDSCAPES

The principles are the same as for painting people and trees, but the emphasis is on details on buildings, such as flowerpots, curtains, pergolas, steps and balconies. Meadows and trees can be painted in the background with plants, fences and farm animals.

The beauty of naive painting is that you don't have to worry about perspective; if you want to paint a cat next to a house, the cat can be the same size as the house, or even bigger. You also don't need to have a frame for your picture if you don't want one. If you feel like it, you could paint one big cat all round the egg!

Finish off the egg with patina (see p. 26) to give it a cheerful appearance.

Icons on eggs

The original icons were religious pictures of the Eastern Orthodox Church painted on wood and, later, on metal.

They were produced primarily for use in churches and for carrying in church processions. The early ones were large in size, but from the 15th century a demand arose for smaller icons, better suited to the smaller private chapels that were being built in Russia at the time. As the Russian people became more prosperous, private ownership of icons became more common, and it became the custom to place an icon in the far-right-hand corner of each room as well as at the head of each bed in the house.

The process of preparing a board for an icon was complicated. The panel first had to be smoothed, then the back had to be strengthened with cut slats. The front was then covered with gesso (plaster of Paris and gypsum), and the canvas was rubbed into the gesso and then finished off with a thin gesso layer. Once it had hardened it had to be polished to produce a very smooth, shiny surface on which the outlines of the picture were sketched, often with red paint. Next the background was applied, usually in gold leaf but sometimes in silver, red, white or green. Only when the background had dried did the painter start on the actual scene, using colours diluted with egg yolk to give the necessary brilliance and opaque effect.

THEMES AND MOTIFS

The traditional icons all had religious themes. You could choose your favourite biblical scene. The important thing is to use the rich and opulent technique to maximum effect.

Materials

Acrylic paint in desired colours
Brushes (number 0, 1, 2 or 3)
Patina set
Craqueleur set
Prepared eggs

Method

1   Nowadays we would paint an icon on an egg in the same manner as a naive picture.
2   Paint the background with white, red or green paint, the colours the Russian people normally used.
3   When the background has dried, trace or draw the rough outlines of your chosen design onto the egg. Paint the outlines with a fine brush and red or brownish-red paint.
4   The painting of the actual scene is almost a ritual, in much the same way as the Chinese tea ceremony. Patience, quiet and love only add to the beauty of the icon, and gold or silver paint complements the design.
5   Once you have completed your picture allow it to dry, then patina the egg for a weathered, antique look. For an even more interesting look, a surface treatment with craqueleur can be done before the patina is applied.
6   Craqueleur consists of two clear lacquers, one slow-drying and the other quick-drying. The slow-drying one is applied first and the other on top of it. Because of the different drying times, stress cracks form on the bottom layer, which creates the effect that the painting (or the egg itself) has cracked. Buy a craqueleur set in a good art shop and use it as directed on the package. Finish with patina.

Delft tradition

Delft is a charming old town in southwestern Holland with beautiful Gothic churches, many Renaissance buildings and winding canals. It is the birthplace of the painter Jan Vermeer (1632-75), who is considered to have been the foremost of the Dutch Old Masters. Since the 17th century Delft has been renowned for its distinctive blue painted and white-glazed porcelain, called 'delfter fayence'. Bottles, vases, jugs, mugs, jars, pots and dishes, as well as the beautiful 'delfter' tiles, are still produced there in this style.

THEMES AND MOTIFS

The most characteristic motifs on traditional delftware are the typical Dutch genre scenes and landscapes, birds, flowers, ships and windmills. Choose a pattern from p. 31 if you don't have one of your own.

The Delft style looks charming when reproduced on eggs, and if you possess some delftware, you could make some eggs to match your collection.

The variations on this theme are endless. You can try dividing the egg in half or quarters, or paint at random round it. You may use the patterns provided in this book, or your own imagination. Look around you – wallpapers, fabrics, etc will give you great ideas.

If you have any Dutch friends, they would particularly appreciate receiving a delft egg as a gift.

Materials

Acrylic paint in two or three shades of blue, and a little black. (I use indigo/prussian blue and ultramarine blue mixed together to get a washy blue.)
Brushes (number 0, 1 or 2)
Tracing materials
Patina set or varnish
Prepared eggs

Method

1 Choose a few immaculate blown eggs and apply two coats of white or slightly off-white paint. The surface should be very smooth and neatly painted.
2 Trace your design onto the egg as described on p. 7. It is best to use dressmaker's carbon paper in a light colour for this because darker coloured carbon paper may smear the delicate white surface.
3 Paint in all the blue sections with your washy-blue mixture, and prepare a second mixture for the darker shades.
4 This time mix the blues and a little black paint with less water and fill in the centres of flowers or one side of buildings where required.
5 When this is dry, mix prussian blue or a similar shade with a little black and paint the outlines with brisk, flourishing strokes, a little away from the blue.
6 Emphasize small details with fine commas to enhance the picture.
7 After finishing one half of the egg, place it carefully on a stand to dry. When it is completely dry, paint the other side.
8 Finish the egg with a varnish paint or spray or oil it (see p. 26).

Geometric and stylised motifs

BLUE-AND-WHITE EGGS

An attractive variation is to have the groundcoat blue and paint white geometric or stylised patterns on the egg. Reversing the colours works equally well – white background and blue patterns. All of the designs should be finished with a varnish spray or cooking oil.

Method

1 Paint a few eggs in a medium blue (ultramarine or cobalt) and some in white. It is important to achieve as smooth a finish as possible.
2 Hold the egg in one hand and, with a fine brush, start to paint (use a contrast colour) round the hole you made for blowing.
3 Taking your time, paint one geometric, ornamental line after another. Don't worry if some of the lines are thicker or thinner than others – handmade objects normally have a few mistakes!
4 After finishing half of the egg, leave it to dry.
5 When it is quite dry, complete the other half.
6 If you tire of geometric patterns, use more stylised designs. Here the egg is divided into halves or quarters, or you may paint round the egg as you see fit. Either use the patterns in this book or create your own designs – wallpaper and fabrics can be very inspiring.

RED-AND-WHITE EGGS

Cadmium red and vermilion eggs look extremely beautiful and are very symbolic. Paint geometric designs on them with a fine brush (number 0).

GREEN-AND-WHITE EGGS

A very interesting effect can be obtained with a plain green background, particularly if you paint freehand with white paint on top of it. As you do not have to concentrate as closely when painting freehand, this method is extremely relaxing.

NATURAL BROWNISH EGGS

Dark brown farm eggs look marvellous if you paint directly onto the shell with black paint, or use waterproof felt-tipped pens.

Calligraphy on eggs

Lettering is an interesting way to embellish your art-work, and you can write the date, a name, a verse of poetry or even a humorous note or message on the egg. The ancient art of calligraphy is a process that requires good basic skills and a lot of practice. Although it is done mostly with a pen, the same technique can be used in brush lettering, the informal italic style being the most suitable for use on eggs.

Materials

Paints as required for background decoration
Thin paint of an inky consistency for calligraphy
Script brush (obtainable at art shops)
Tracing materials
Varnish
Prepared eggs

Method 1 – with a script brush

1 Divide the egg in two with a border of commas or dots and decide where you want to place the letters and the other elements of the design.

2 Finish off all the other artwork before you start on the script.
3 Using the alphabet below, trace the message onto tracing paper. Now transfer this onto the egg surface using carbon or graphite paper. Bear in mind that the letters should be uniformly spaced.
4 With enough practice you will be able to do the letters freehand.
5 Hold the brush at a 45° angle to the baseline when you apply the lettering.
6 When you have completed it, apply varnish to highlight and protect your work.

Method 2 – with a felt-tipped pen

1 An quick and easy way to do lettering on your egg is to use a Rexel calligraphy felt-tipped pen (obtainable at stationery shops).
2 For script on a normal-sized egg a number 2 size should be suitable.
3 Copy the letters freehand from a sketch, allow to dry and varnish with a spray to protect and enhance the lettering.

Scratching, etching, blocking and batik

Decorating eggs with these techniques is a very old tradition in many countries, particularly in Eastern Europe. Women used to sit with their children, scratching and etching until perfection had been reached. It was a very time-consuming but satisfying activity, so what better way to explore the old folk arts than with this timeless and restful decorative method.

SCRATCHING

This consists of using a pointed instrument to scratch a design onto the surface of a dyed egg.

Materials

Tool for scratching (penknife, razor blade or nailfile)
Prepared eggs already dyed in the colours of your choice

Method

1   Use a white, thick- and smooth-shelled egg that has been dyed a very intense colour. Try a hard-boiled egg to begin with.
2   Hold the egg with a paper towel, draw or trace a design on the surface, then start scratching with your sharp tool.
3   Scratch along the lines of the design, but be careful when you scratch near the blowing holes if you are using a blown egg. If you are a beginner you should start by scratching only simple designs, and use dark-coloured eggs only.

ETCHING

In this technique you draw a design on a brightly coloured egg with a pen that has been dipped in acid.

Materials

Prepared eggs already dyed in the colours of your choice (greater contrast is achieved by using eggs in dark colours)
Acid solution (use either citric acid: 30 g powder in one teaspoon water, or a 3% solution of hydrochloric acid, obtainable from a pharmacy. If you use the latter be extremely careful; it is very poisonous.)
Nib pen, toothpick or sharpened goose feather
Absorbent cloth
Tracing materials

Method

1   Trace your design onto the surface of the egg.
2   Dip the pen into the acid, and follow the drawing lines on the surface of the egg.
3   Wipe off the excess acid at once with the absorbent cloth; the pattern appears in soft, unblurred lines.
4   Once finished, rinse the egg and apply either varnish spray or a drop of oil to give it a shiny look.

BLOCKING

For this ancient method small flowers, leaves, pieces of material and tiny paper cutouts can be used.

Materials

Dyes in required colours
Flowers, leaves, material, etc for blocking
Nylon stocking
Egg white or cooking oil
Prepared eggs

Method

1   Lightly dip the objects you want to use in cooking oil or egg white and arrange them on an uncoloured, prepared egg.
2   Wrap the egg tightly in the nylon stocking and secure at both ends with thread, so the blocked objects are pressed firmly aginst the shell.
3   Dye the egg in the colour bath and when dry remove the nylon stocking and blocked objects. The egg will retain their imprint.

BATIK

We all associate batik with fabric – not many people are aware that using the batik technique on eggs is an old decorating tradition.

You can batik an egg by drawing a design on the uncoloured egg with melted wax. The egg is what will

be dyed afterwards. The procedure can be repeated several times, starting with light shades and moving on to darker ones.

Materials

One to five bowls of dye
Pins in various sizes, stuck into wood or cork
Wax (the best type is beeswax, which can be bought
  ready-mixed)
Small bowl or spoon
Candle
Well-cleaned eggs (wiped with vinegar to remove all
  traces of grease)

Method

1   Place a small amount of wax in the bowl (or spoon) and heat it in a water-bath or over a candle flame until it has melted but not boiled.
2   Dip a pinhead (a goose quill or nib pen can also be used) into the melted wax and touch it quickly to the egg to form a dot, comma or line.

3   You must dip your tool into the wax before doing each stroke of the design. It is a good idea to practise first on a small piece of eggshell.
4   When you are satisfied with the result, place the egg in the prepared dye bath. To achieve an even colour make sure the bath is warm, but not more than 40 °C, or the wax may melt away.
5   Once you have removed the egg from the bath, dry it with a soft cloth.
6   Remove the wax only if you want a one-coloured batik. To do this, hold the egg against the side of a candle flame (keep it away from the top of the flame or you will end up with soot marks on the egg).
7   Wipe the wax away with an absorbent cloth as soon as it melts.
8   If you would like a multicoloured batik, leave the wax on after the first dye bath. Once the egg is dry, add more wax and dye the egg again.
9   This procedure can be repeated a few times, but you must always work from light to dark shades. Start with yellow, then move on to red, blue, violet and black.
10   Remove the wax layers only after the last colour bath. Polish the finished eggs with a drop of cooking oil.

Easter and other festive occasions

EGGS FOR EASTER

Easter has a cheerful tradition. The name is derived from 'Eostre', the Germanic goddess of dawn. Easter Sunday and Monday sunrises were greeted with dancing, fun and games. In many villages in Austria, for example, Easter Sunday always started in the early hours, with cannons being fired with loud and joyful noisiness. Children strolled through gardens and houses, hunting for the Easter nest, a nest full of good things from the Easter bunny.

Legend has it that the rabbit was the favourite animal of Eostre. Because the rabbit, like the egg, has always been closely associated with fertility and growth, it has become one of the most well-known symbols of Easter. In the Northern hemisphere this occurs at the beginning of Spring. Since the 16th century children have believed that the rabbit brings the Easter eggs. They often build 'nests' in their gardens to lure the rabbit.

Another Christian custom is to paint cooked eggs and take them, together with bread and meat neatly packed in a basket, to the church on Easter Saturday to be blessed by the priest in remembrance of the resurrection of Jesus Christ. This custom is still practised today, and all over the world it forms one of the most important parts of the Easter celebrations. On Easter Sunday, the colourful eggs are the decorative highlights of the table.

After the religious and culinary celebration of Easter Sunday, Easter Monday has always been kept for fun and games with the eggs. It seems that every ancient civilization had its own rituals and games, including egg-tossing, egg-tapping and egg-dancing.

The 'toss-an-egg' game provided a source of income for male youngsters. The performers dressed up and painted their faces, then strolled in small groups from farmhouse to farmhouse, trying to persuade the occupants to toss eggs into their baskets. A most welcome substitute was money. Afterwards they enacted a play or sang a song in return for the contribution.

Egg-tapping was a popular game in many countries. Old and young alike used cooked and decorated Easter eggs to damage their opponents' eggs in duel-like combat. The owner of the undamaged egg was declared the winner.

Egg-dancing was performed by dancing between some eggs while blindfolded, trying not to trample any.

If the dancer succeeded in his or her effort, prize money was forthcoming, and for the villagers it was lots of fun to watch.

The main attraction at Easter is the egg-painting and egg-giving tradition. Prepare well in advance, blowing and painting eggs, and decorate your home with garlands, wreaths and stands decorated with lovely painted eggs.

Traditionally everyone I meet during Easter week receives a painted egg from me. To be prepared for this occasion, I have lots of cooked and blown eggs in a basket to be handed out as little gifts of friendship.

All the friendly and often surprised smiles and thanks one receives are very rewarding, and strengthen existing bonds of friendship. It is an especially joyful event when eggs are painted and decorated by the whole family. This ritual is most comforting and enhances family bonds.

EGGS FOR CHRISTMAS

Not only are eggs suitable for Easter, they are also used on numerous other occasions. In some parts of Belgium, the Christmas tree is traditionally decorated with eggs painted with elegant gold and silver backgrounds, seasonal or religious motifs or Father Christmas.

I have painted a number of Christmas eggs myself and the results are surprising different and beautiful. I merely applied glue to parts of the shells, then rolled them in salt. After this dried I painted some of the eggs, covering random areas with colour. I used artist's acrylic paint in silver and very little blue on some eggs, and gold with a touch of green on others.

After the paint dried I finished the eggs with a varnish spray. These egg decorations make any Christmas tree extra special.

SPECIAL OCCASIONS

There is a renewed interest in arts and crafts, probably as a reaction to the uniformity of mass-produced articles. Egg-painting is one of the old crafts enjoying a revival, and painted eggs make the most delightful, personal gifts. They can be decorated for numerous occasions and special events such as birthdays, anniversaries, weddings and the birth of a baby.

Finishing and presentation

FINISHING

After the egg has been dyed or painted as required you should finish it to protect it. Rub it with a drop of cooking oil, an easy, old-fashioned way to add lustre to the colours.

You may also use the patina technique, which is widely used for eggs decorated in the folk art, Bauernmalerei, icon or naive methods. Roll a piece of non-fluffy cloth into a ball and squeeze 1 mm of burnt umber artist's oil colour onto it. Dip the ball into a mixture of one part linseed oil and two parts turpentine and cover the surface of the egg with a layer of the compound.

Wipe the egg once again, removing most of the brownish patina. You will find the shading that results from the application of the compound will give the egg a slightly weathered look. When it is completely dry, after about 12 hours, the patina will give the same protection as a varnish, with the advantage that the paint-work on the egg is not sealed off from the air.

With some techniques it is preferable to spray the egg with a varnish for protection and shine rather than use patina.

PRESENTATION

If you are going to take the trouble to decorate an egg beautifully, you should take as much trouble to ensure that it is presented or displayed attractively. Here are some ideas for finishing and presenting your eggs.

Ribbon, bows and thread

If your decorated egg has only one hole, tie a thread onto a matchstick and push it through the hole. Use the thread to hang the egg from an appropriate place – a palm tree, a straw, cane or green wreath, a pot plant, fresh or dry flowers, a dry arrangement in a vase or anywhere that it can be displayed to full advantage.

If the egg has two holes you can thread a length of ribbon right through it. Fasten one or two beads or tie a bow at one end to make sure it stays in place.

Eggs on stands

You can use curtain rings, candle holders or egg holders as stands for decorated eggs, or make a suitable stand to show the egg off – especially the striking ostrich egg – to best advantage.

Eggs on sticks

Stand the egg on a small wooden skewer which you can paint in the same colour. Place a bead on one side and a bow on the other. Place the stick in a vase or pot plant to show it off to best effect.

Egg garland

Prepare six or eight eggs (with two holes) and then pull a thread through all of them, a bead between each. Tie the ends of the thread together to form a garland. This makes a wonderful decoration to hang in a window or door, or on a wall. It can also be used as a centrepiece on a table for dinner parties and special occasions. Why not make one especially for your festive Easter dinner table?

Containers for eggs

Unpacking a gift usually gives just as much pleasure as the gift itself, especially when the outside of the package looks just as good as the contents. If you are giving a decorated egg as a gift, make sure the wrapping is just as attractive as the egg inside. It looks lovely if the egg and container are painted in the same style or show some similarity in colour or design.

If you are looking for an unusual container, try the traditional German *Spanschachtel*, a wooden gift box usually obtainable at German bookshops. This box is made of very thinly planed 'slices' of wood and is rather fragile.

But you don't have to buy a container especially for your egg – look round your house for suitable boxes such as children's shoeboxes or any other suitably sized cardboard boxes.

With a little imagination you can turn the plainest box into a beautiful presentation pack.

A really attractive presentation idea is to make a nest out of dry vines and add a collection of different bird feathers with one or more painted eggs. The effect is stunning – and the nest is pretty enough to serve as a permanent container for displaying the eggs.

Techniques for children

BATIK

Let the child drip wax from a burning candle onto the egg. Make sure you supervise this operation very closely! By turning the egg he or she can create an abstract design of dots and stripes.

Allow the wax to dry and dip the egg into a colour bath. The process can be repeated with different colour baths if the child wants a multicoloured effect.

When the egg is finished remove the wax by heating it at the side of a candle flame and wiping it away as it melts.

WAX DRIPPING

With this method children can melt odds and ends of wax crayons in a candle flame and then drip them onto a white or dyed egg. In this case, however, the wax is the decoration and remains on the egg.

PRINTING

Potato printing is an easy way to make personalized eggs for all occasions. Do you remember doing potato printing at school? It is a versatile and simple way for children to decorate eggs.

Prepare the printing blocks from pieces of potato: for leaves and flowers cut the potato in half lengthways; for small leaves and flowers cut it widthways. Use a pencil to engrave a design on the potato. Spread the paint, which can be acrylic or poster paint, thinly on a large dinner plate and let the children dip their printing blocks into it. Wipe the potato pieces with a paper towel before starting because they must not be too wet.

The key to carving potatoes is to remember that what you cut away will remain white, and what is left will print your colour.

BLOCKING

This technique is described on p. 22. It is great fun as a family project. Use natural ingredients, listed on p. 6, to make children aware of how useful nature is in providing harmless and readily available colours.

SPONGING

This method (described on p. 8) is particularly popular with children. Let them sponge more than one colour onto the egg.

PAINTING WITH KOKI PENS, PASTELS AND CRAYONS

Children should round up a collection of crayons, pastels and koki (felt-tipped) pens from their drawing boxes. Using hard-boiled or blown eggs they can draw or 'colour in' any design they like.

ETCHING

This form of egg decoration (described on p. 22) is also suitable for children, but substitute a milder acid solution such as vinegar.

The process will take a little longer but the effects will be the same.

Patterns

DIVIDING UP THE SURFACE

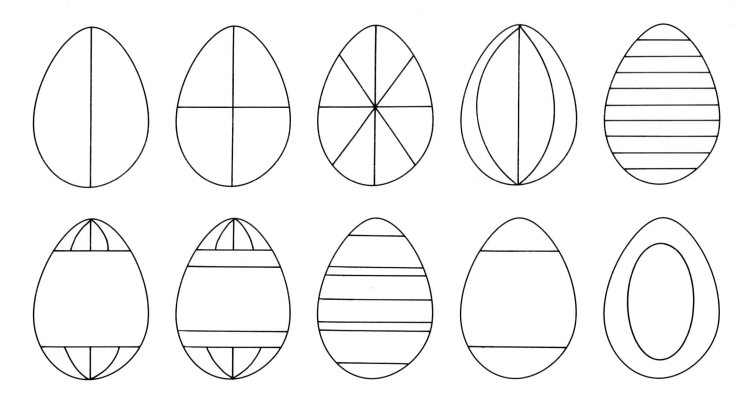

'POLES' OF EGGS (i.e. top and bottom)

BAUERNMALEREI, NAIVE AND DELFT MOTIFS

'SIDES' OF EGGS

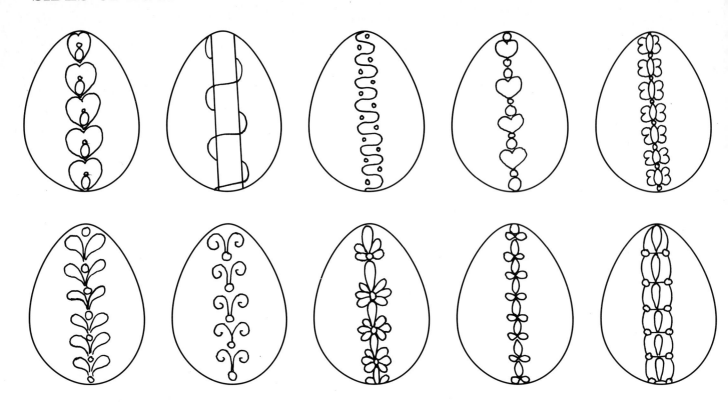

GEOMETRIC AND STYLISED MOTIFS